HOW TO
DRAW & PAINT
LANDSCAPES

A QUINTET BOOK

Published by Chartwell Books Inc.,
A Division of Book Sales Inc.,
110 Enterprise Avenue,
Secaucus, New Jersey 07094

ISBN 1-55521-051-1

This book was designed and produced by
Quintet Publishing Limited
6 Blundell Street, London N7

Editorial Director: Jeremy Harwood
Art Director: Robert Morley
Editors: Victoria Funk, Judy Martin
Art Editor: Neville Graham

Printed in Hong Kong by Leefung-Asco
Printers Limited

HOW TO DRAW & PAINT
LANDSCAPES

CONTENTS

Landscape

THE NATURAL ENVIRONMENT of man is bound to be a popular subject used in paintings and drawings. Earlier art, however, tended to stress the narrative elements of the picture and landscape was often relegated to the background. Indeed, so important was the priority given to man and animal that often a landscape was no more than a cypher, meriting no reference at all.

Egyptian artists used reeds and skies, creating an atmosphere in which birds, beasts and fishes could exist. These landscapes are less descriptions of specific places than arrangements of separate landscape elements, cunningly disposed in order to relate as parts of the overall picture. Thus, a clump of bullrushes are placed on the surface at a calculated distance from the birds living and nesting in them.

The growth of landscape
The use of the component parts of landscape to symbolize the environment and the adjustment of the landscape to make it conform to the design needs of the picture has persisted. It would of course be remarkable if trees, hills, shrubs and clouds all perfectly interlocked into foreground, animals, figures and the like. The French 17th century painter Poussin is a fine example of an 'orchestrated' landscapist, with each element playing its part, not merely to establish space for the subject of the painting, but also allowing shapes, colors, and textures to contribute to the painting's overall effect.

From humble beginnings, the landscape came to be used as a major part of the picture and indeed to eventually become the whole of the picture. The painters of Renaissance Italy in depicting Biblical events used the everyday scenes around them for the church-goer to identify with. Because the streets of the cities and the forested hills beyond were an unquestioned part of everyday life, great historic dramas were enacted within these pictures, the better to be understood by the common man.

Since the 17th century, landscape painting has flourished and we now think of several interpreters of the fields, seas, and mountains as amongst the greatest of artists. Atmospheric painters such as William Turner, John Constable, and Edward Hopper employed the principles of both linear and atmospheric perspective, and the engravings of Rembrandt and others show a similar knowledge.

It is advisable to plot with care the composition of your landscape, for certainly anyone painting such a subject, whether from life or from sketches, will have to make adjustments to the natural scene. Nature herself will be perfect when viewed as a landscape, but a piece of it trapped within a rectangle or square as a picture will certainly contain unwanted elements. Be prepared to remove, substitute, or add a tree; feel free to reduce the amount of yellow if it seems to jump out of context, and to mix a range of greens rather than use one basic green, even if such a basic green is modified by other colours. The source of such greens – Prussian blue plus yellow or viridian green – will show if too much of it appears in the same area. Brown and blue will also offer a new green to the palette; always experiment as our demonstrations set out to suggest.

Landscape media
When working in watercolors or gouache, the principle of varying the basic green used is again of great importance. Because these pictures are likely to be small in scale, several important decisions must be taken before committing the paint to paper, especially in watercolor painting. This often demands an analytical attitude, deciding which colors to use in order to simplify things and then modifying one layer with another, as brilliantly exemplified in the pictures of Girtman and Cotman, both 19th century artists.

With gouache, the problems differ for one can overpaint, make adjustments, even pile paint on very thickly for particular effects, as seen in the work of Samuel Palmer (1805–1881).

Pen and ink suits landscape interpretation, as it has a conciseness and fineness of detail that gives the subject a good feeling. Never hesitate

Surface shapes The most common shapes are landscape and portrait. Landscapes need not be horizontal nor portraits vertical.

Samuel Palmer, 'In a Shoreham Garden'. This painting is a good example of the unique qualities of gouache used in landscape painting. Note as well the incorporation of the figure in an otherwise purely natural picture showing how landscape and figure subjects can be successfully combined.

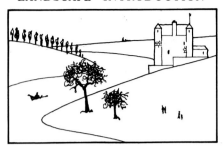

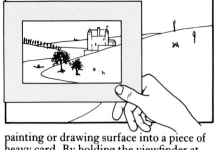

The viewfinder A viewfinder can be a great help in choosing a suitable composition. The viewer is made by cutting a shape similar to that of the painting or drawing surface into a piece of heavy card. By holding the viewfinder at arm's length, the artist can select the view of the scene to be used.

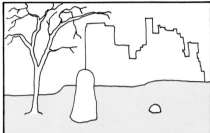

Strengthening composition The composition of a picture is often determined by the goal of the artist. For example, if an accurate rendering of a scene is desired, the artist will move about to find the most interesting point of view. If, however, the artist is more concerned with the painting itself rather than a realistic rendition of the scene, he may use creative license to rearrange objects. Left: The picture is pleasing but uninteresting. Right: Interest is added by moving the tree to the right and introducing another element.

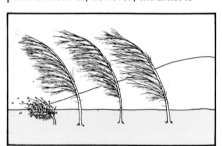

Motion and direction Left: Objects in a landscape are susceptible to the elements of nature and not least of these is wind. When movement is involved, it should be looked for in all objects, not just the obvious. Right: In this picture, the road leads the observer's eye across the picture plane. The idea of leading the eye through the use of direction is an important element in all types of painting and drawing.

The sky In all landscape work, the sky can be used as either a major or minor pictorial element – but it will always influence the rest of the picture. Above: Loose, billowing cloud shapes are emphasized by the straight, hard horizon line. Center: Using a very high horizon line and only a small indication of land, a semi-abstract image is achieved. Right: The sky is an effective backdrop for the sharp outline of the castle, creating a silhouette effect.

William Turner, 'Stormy Sea with Blazing Wreck

to use any outside aid such as the ruler for there is no great achievement in putting unreasonable handicaps in your way and ruled lines will contrast very well with the freely drawn line. Splattering ink, using unlikely instruments – string dipped in ink or the edge of a piece of wood or plastic – will add to the range of textures and therefore to the possibilities.

...rner was a master at creating stimulating land and seascapes. In this picture, paint has been heavily impasted to build up rich, subtle tones.

Pencil drawing has been used a great deal for this subject in recent times, and the 20th century artist Paul Hogarth has shown an astonishing freshness and variety of touch in his drawings of buildings, landscapes, and city streets. This is achieved by using a number of pencils and often consolidating the drawing by adding ink to emphasize details.

The sky is a constant element in any landscape interpretation whether drawn or painted. Be aware of it as not merely a backdrop to the scene but as an integral part, able to lend drama through heavy clouds or suggest vastness by being indicated as a simple void. Constable made many small sketches in color of changing skies, cloud masses, etc. and was able to

incorporate things learned from these into his larger pictures. Because the source of light will generally be in the sky, it follows that in most cases it will be the lightest tone in the landscape. However, do not let it disassociate itself from the remainder of the piece but integrate it into your overall scheme by adjusting either it or the land mass.

Colour & Perspective

Color

It is necessary to study some of the basic theories of picture making and this includes perhaps the most basic, but not necessarily the simplest of all: color. No matter what other features paintings have, the common factor in all is color. Indeed, in the normally sighted human being, what is actually seen is the many and varied sensations of color. The retina of the eye receives sensations from objects which causes a reaction in the appropriate cones. As a result, trees appear green because the cones that have green as their dominant assert themselves and overcome the cones that have other colours. Similarly, the blue of the sky, is caused by the receiving of 'blue' pulses into the retina which immediately triggers a reaction to the blue-stressed cones. In color blindness these cones go wrong and often colors are reversed.

Since this complex act of seeing happens only within the brain, it is correct to deduce that nothing has color in its own right but that color is dependent upon light. In darkened conditions, colors are more difficult to see and define, and in total darkness there can be no color at all. An interesting experiment is that of creating an after-image in the retina demonstrating that it is through the brain that color is seen. Stare at a red patch, then shut your eyes and 'look' at the after-image. The same shape is seen, but in green – the complementary colour of the red patch.

Complementary colors are those at opposite sides of the color wheel. One of these colors, in this case red, reacts through the red cones and the other through the green. Taking complementary colors, we can see that a knowledge of this aspect of color theory is of value when we consider landscape painting.

In an average landscape painting, most areas are of greens of one sort or another. Brilliant, dull, acid; sage, spring, olive or sea, man has created descriptions for various conditions and types of green. If our painting comprises fields, shrubs, trees, and bushes all made up of these various greens, how better to make the harmony complete than by contrasting a

The color wheel. Color has been the subject of study for many hundreds of years ranging from the simple act of observation to highly complex psychophysical theories. In terms of painting and drawing, some of the most important terms include hue, tone, and warm and cool colors. *Hue* is the range seen in the color wheel. The *Tone* refers to the brightness of a color. *Warm and cool* colors describe the orange and blue sections of the color wheel, respectively.

Additive mixture. Red, green and blue are known as additive primaries. When two of these are combined a third color is created which is the complement of the third color.

Subtractive mixture. When two additive colors are combined they create a subtractive color. The colors produced are cyan, yellow, and magenta. When white light is passed through, black is created.

small amount of the opposite, or complementary color, being, in this instance, red. The red will serve to enhance the values of the main body of color – the range of subtly mixed greens. To expand this, since we know that green is a secondary color created from two primary colors (blue and yellow), we can begin to see how this can aid us as well. A similar effect to placing small areas of red beside the green will be created by using blue and yellow in a like manner. By using brilliant Prussian blue and raw umber or raw sienna instead of yellow, an unsuspected green tint will result. Further experimentation will reveal all manner of exciting relationships, not merely of color values – that is 'blueness' or 'redness' – but also of qualities and tones.

Tone and hue
Color has two basic definable qualities: tone and hue. Hue is the

'greenness' of green paint, and tone is its darkness or lightness. Squinting is indispensable in assessing color tones when beginning to work and throughout the painting's development. Expressionistic color as used by 20th century artists such as Matisse and Derain, or the more traditional use as seen in Velazquez (17th century) are worthy of close study. In studying paintings, try always to detach the color element from the whole painting in order to examine it the better.

There is little point in simply copying 'color as seen' without attempting to first organize a scheme. Whether the artist's intention is to shock or to create a mood strictly with a number of tertiary colors, forethought is essential. One method of studying color is to use sheets of specially colored papers, cut out and placed in various shapes and combinations to see what happens when tones are too close or too distant.

Perspective

What is a good picture? There is no simple answer; perhaps one that excites or disturbs, not one necessarily pleasing to the eye, but containing a great deal of visual interest. Not only should the artist be facile in his knowledge and use of the materials, but he or she should be conversant with these other important ingredients of visual communication and, through the fusion of these various elements, achieve his or her ambitions.

In picture making, the elements every artist needs to understand in order to best exploit them include color, composition, and perspective. The fusion of these components with a good basic drawing ability and sound technique give the artist an opportunity to express his personal vision.

These aspects of painting and drawing can be sufficiently learned to allow

One, two, and three point perspective. When two planes are visible, the parallel lines converge at a single vanishing point. When three planes are visible, two points are required. If a cube is seen above or below the horizon line, three points are used.

Seeing. The human eye functions in a highly complex system allowing us to view the world in three dimensions. Distance is formulated by the angle of convergence of the image on the retina. When many objects are viewed, sophisticated computations take place in the brain.

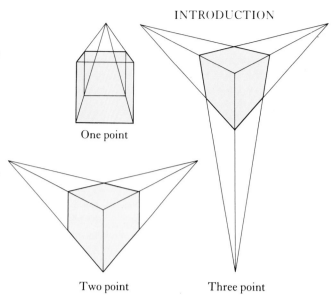

One point

Two point

Three point

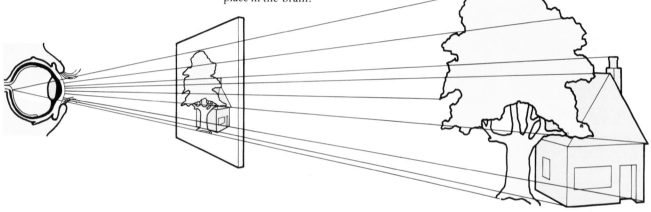

Pieter Bruegel, 'The Fall of Icarus'. The concept of aerial perspective is clearly shown in this painting. Notice how objects close up are precise and detailed and those in the middle and far distance become hazy and less well defined.

the original inspiration, no matter how ambitious, to ultimately be resolved. Systematic plotting, allied with an assertion of the artist's intention is the way to achieve good results. No one, however, should expect to always attain their highest levels of work. Being prepared to accept that the 'near

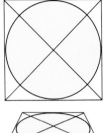

Spherical perspective. Top: If one were to visualize this shape as a teacup seen from the top, as the viewer sits down, the circle becomes an ellipse. To create an ellipse, enclose a circle in a square, bisect it, connect diagonals, and draw ellipse.

miss', the 'brave attempt', or even the outright failure is the sign of a good student. Experience and the ambition to push things a bit beyond one's reach is productive, sound reasoning.

Along with linear perspective, the artist uses aerial or atmospheric perspective. Aerial perspective is that which deals with the reduction and changes of tones and colors due to the distance between them and the viewer. A formula used in the past, e.g., by Pieter Bruegel (c.1525–1569) in 'The Fall of Icarus', demonstrates the basic idea of aerial perspective. Objects close-up are seen to be in full tonal and color values; bright, light surfaces facing the light source, and dark in those turned away. Objects

seen at a short distance, behind these objects, can be seen to have a less well defined distinction between their light and dark sides.

In atmospheric perspective, colors will be seen to have been modified by the atmosphere and to take on a bluish tone. In the middle distance, this is more marked with less subject definition and closer color values, and so on until, in the far distance, only the shape of objects can be discerned and the blue so assertive that things appear to be pure blue. This use of the dark brown foreground, green middle distance, and blue far-distance was in common use in the 17th and 18th centuries. No such rigid formula is to be encouraged, but the use of aerial perspective is essential in the type of work under discussion.

The simplest demonstration of the problems encountered by anyone attempting to transfer a sphere on to a two-dimensional surface is seen in that of two-dimensional projections of the earth. One can begin to see that the point of using such a system of perspective is simply to allow the picture to tell its intended truth. The artist, however, must understand the limitation of such theories well enough to be prepared to depart from the rules as much as needed.

This is of course a direct corollary to the embracing of any scientific method be it of color, perspective, or proportions. They are very useful as servants, potentially disastrous as masters. The one constant criterion in all picture making is the intention and content of the work undertaken; all other considerations are dependent upon this. A good artist is prepared to use all, or none, of these systems towards this end.

Aerial perspective. In general, objects in space diminish in tone as they recede from the viewer and those closest appear darkest. This, however, is not a hard and fast rule as many conditions will affect this principle such as the source of light, the brightness of objects and their reflected light. Tonal variations should be carefully studied rather than preconceived.

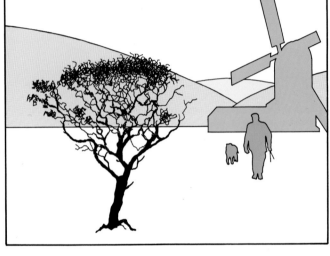

Linear and aerial perspective. The combination of linear perspective (the path) and aerial perspective (the diminishing tones of the receding trees) combine to create a sense of depth. Leonardo da Vinci created aerial perspective as a means to describe the different visible tones of objects in space. Objects viewed at a distance will appear to take on a bluish tone due to the scattering of light waves.

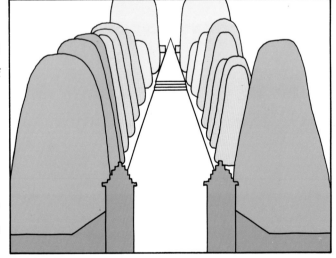

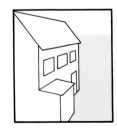 

The horizon line. The horizon line is always at eye level. No matter what the size or dimensions of objects, their diagonal lines will all converge on the horizon line.

To visualize the scale of a painting, when studying the techniques used, each of the pictures shown from pages 14 to 61 are illustrated on a small grid to show their relative size. The maximum size being 39in × 30in (97cm × 75cm), each square in the grid represents 3in (7.5cm). The relative size of the painting is indicated by the tinted area.

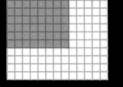

Albrecht Durer: The Monumental Turf. Durer was the first major artist to use water colour.

Oil

THERE ARE VARIOUS ways of undertaking the preparatory stages of an oil painting. Here the composition is roughly outlined using a soft pencil; this method requires a light touch as heavy pressure may dent the canvas and cause the stretched surface to sag. The composition is divided roughly in half, but the artist has taken care to avoid making a completely symmetrical division of the picture plane, as this would interfere with the spatial illusion.

The low wall and brightly lit garden urn on the left of the painting underline the horizontal emphasis but, more importantly, provide a focal point which contrasts with the large expanse of green. The result is to create an overall sense of harmony. The shades of green are varied by the addition of blue, white, yellow and red.

The texture of the surface was enlivened by spattering wet paint from the end of the brush and constantly altering the directions of the brushstrokes. The best way to apply the paint is to vary the techniques; for instance, lay thin glazes over patches of solid color, scrub the paint into the weave of the canvas, and feather the brushstrokes into textured trails.

Materials

Surface
Stretched, primed canvas

Size
39in × 30in (98cm × 75cm)

Tools
1in decorator's brush
Nos 6 and 8 hog bristle brushes
No 8 round sable brush
Wooden artist's palette

Colors

Black	Cobalt blue
Burnt sienna	Chrome green
Burnt umber	White
Cadmium red	Yellow ochre
Cadmium yellow	

Medium
Turpentine

1. Draw up the composition lightly in pencil. Block in a loose impression of the background shapes with thin paint. Use greens with blue, yellow and red.

3. Lay in a solid expanse of chrome green across the whole of the foreground, using a 1in (2.5 cm) decorator's brush.

5. Work over the colors with fine linear brushmarks and thin layers of dribbled and spattered paint to increase the variety of tone and texture.

7. Work over the whole image making slight adjustments to the shapes and colors. Bring up the light tones and darken shadows.

2. Continue to develop the shapes, varying the tonal contrasts and breaking up the color masses with linear brushmarks and small patches of different hues.

4. Work over the sky and around the forms of the trees with a thick layer of light blue. Draw back into the green shapes with the brush to make the outline more intricate.

6. Define the shape of the wall with small dabs of brown, red and pink laid against strong black shadows. Blend and soften the color with a dry brush.

8. Brush in a thick layer of bright green over the right of the foreground, working into the dark shadow area to bring out the illusion of light and shade.

Details of wall · outlining the urn redefining tree outlines

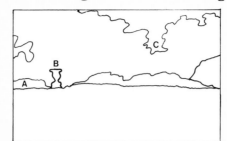

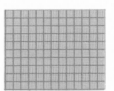

A. With a small sable brush, the artist is here putting in details in the wall. The previous layer was allowed to dry thoroughly before overpainting.

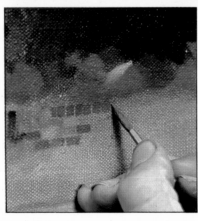

B. With a small bristle brush, the artist is here working carefully around the urn to strengthen outlines.

C. With a small sable brush and a thickish mixture of pale blue paint, the artist works back into the tree shapes.

IN ALL PAINTING and drawing, the artist's decision on what media and techniques he or she uses to create a picture is a highly individual and selective process. The factors involved are a combination of practical skill, an understanding of the media and techniques and, most importantly, how the artist sees the picture in his or her mind's eye.

In this picture the *alla prima* method has been used. This is a quick, direct method of painting which can be used to create a bold and exciting picture in a short period of time. From a rough sketch, the artist works directly on to the surface, as opposed to the traditional method of building up layer upon layer of color, or working from dark to light. In unskilled hands, this sometimes can be risky as in laying down thick, heavy areas of paint, the artist is often simply hoping that the result will reflect the initial intention. When working as heavily as this, the main danger is of either building up the paint surface too quickly or mistakenly putting down wrong colors. However, one of the beauties of oil paint is that it can be easily scraped off and the artist can begin again.

To work with bold color requires a good color sense and a knowledge of how the individual colors interact with one another. Here, the artist has used 'unnatural' colors such as purples, greens, and reds over basic earth tones to both preserve the feeling of the subject and add interest and variety to the painting.

Materials

Surface
Prepared canvas board

Size
24in × 20in (60cm × 50cm)

Tools
Nos 2 and 4 flat bristle brushes
Palette
Palette knife
Rags or tissues
Willow charcoal

Colors

Burnt umber	Permanent magenta
Cadmium red light	Prussian blue
Cadmium yellow light	Raw sienna
Cadmium yellow	Raw umber
Cobalt blue	Yellow ochre
French ultramarine	White

Medium
Turpentine

1. After lightly sketching in the subject with willow charcoal, apply a thin wash of general color areas in cool and warm tones with a No 4 bristle brush.

2. With burnt sienna and cadmium yellow, overlay the roughed-in areas with thick, short strokes of color, using the stroke to define the shapes.

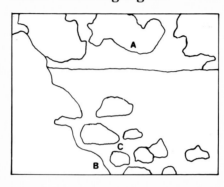

3. Build up the dark tones with Prussian blue and burnt umber and lighter 'dark' tones in green. Add touches of cadmium red as highlight areas.

4. Develop the light areas with cadmium yellow, ochre, red, and purple mixed from ultramarine blue and magenta. Develop water with Prussian blue.

5. Using a No 2 bristle brush, continue to lay in the water highlights in cadmium yellow and white, allowing the underpainting to show through.

Cloud texture · modelling rocks · water highlights

A. The artist is here putting in cloud shapes with a thick, opaque paint mixture and a small bristle brush.

B. Allowing colors to mix directly on the surface, the artist puts in thick strokes of paint in the rocks, allowing previous layers to show through.

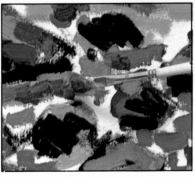

C. With a small bristle brush, various tones are touched into the water area to create a rippled texture.

THE MAIN TECHNIQUE demonstrated in this painting is considered particularly suitable for landscapes involving broad planes of color. The paint is applied thickly with a knife in simple shapes and, as a result, details emerge from the paint surface, rather than being dictated by the structure of the drawing. The composition is built up with overlaid layers of impasto paint giving a craggy, ridged texture. Each individual shape has a ragged edge where small vestiges of previous layers break through the top coat of color. In the final stages the work is coated with very thin, liquid glazes of color. These settle into the pitted impasto to form a veined sheen over the surface, drawing the tones together.

The limited range of color serves to focus attention on the texture of the paint, as does the simplicity of the composition. The balance of tone, color and texture is achieved by continual adjustment of the paint mixtures. The technique must be carefully controlled because the paint is thick and wet – frequent drying out periods may be needed before further layers can be added. Use palette knives to lay in thick paint areas and spread glazes with a clean rag to work the color into the surface.

Materials

Surface
Stretched, primed canvas

Size
12in × 9in (30cm × 22.5cm)

Tools
Palette knives: short trowel, 3in (7.5cm) cranked blade, 3in (7.5cm) straight blade; palette; rags or tissues

Colors
Paint:	*Pastels:*
Alizarin crimson	Black
Black	Cerulean blue
Cerulean blue	Ultramarine blue
Payne's grey	Yellow ochre
Prussian blue	
White	

Mediums
Linseed oil
Turpentine

1. Lay a wash of thin grey oil paint over the whole canvas, rubbing it in with a clean rag. Draw up the basic lines of the composition with oil pastels.

2. Apply thick layers of paint with a palette knife, blocking in the shapes with light blues, grey and mauve.

3. Still using the palette knife, build up the textured surface, lightening the tones of the colors. Work in broad, directional sweeps of broken color.

4. Continue to lay in grey and blue tones, varying the direction of the strokes.

5. Heighten the colors, working over the central shapes with solid white and light greys. Allow the underlayers to show through the thick paint.

6. Adjust the tones over the whole work to warm up the color balance. Even out the colors but keep the thick impasto quality.

Underpainting · painting with palette knife

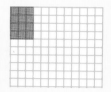

The artist blocks in general color areas with a palette knife, using a thick, opaque mixture of paint.

A thin ground of grey paint and turpentine has been rubbed into the canvas. On top of this the artist puts in the general outlines of the composition in oil pastel.

Draw the knife across the surface, blending the paint well into the canvas with even consistent strokes.

MANY ARTISTS FIND that working from photographs is an acceptable way of creating landscapes. However, there are disadvantages. Although the method enables an artist to increase his or her range of subject matter, it is limiting in terms of a fixed viewpoint and static lighting. The artist can compensate for this by exploiting colors and textures of the painting and by developing aspects of the image which naturally attract attention.

In this painting, the warm glow of light and pattern of trees and flowers have been exaggerated and used as the basis for a more colorful interpretation of the subject. The bright pastel colors of the sky are echoed in the pathway through the center of the picture, while the predominance of green has been enlivened by adding red, forming a contrast of complementary colors.

You can experiment with brushwork, laying the paint on quite thickly; oil paint can be scraped off and the surface reworked if an area of the painting is unsuccessful. Use three or four different brush shapes and sizes and vary the strokes between the tip and flat of the bristles. If necessary, let the painting dry out for a few days before completing the final stages, so that clear colors and clean whites can be laid over the darker tones.

Materials

Surface
Prepared canvas board

Size
24in × 20in (60cm × 50cm)

Tools
2B pencil
Nos 3 and 5 flat bristle brushes
No 1 round bristle brush
No 4 filbert bristle brush
Palette

Colors
Alizarin crimson	Cobalt blue
Black	Hooker's green
Cadmium green	Terre verte
Cadmium red	Ultramarine blue
Cadmium yellow	Violet
Chrome orange	White

Medium
Turpentine

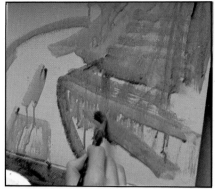

1. After sketching in the composition, with a very thin wash of green and turpentine, quickly block in main shapes with a large, soft sable brush.

2. Load a bristle brush with cadmium green well thinned with turpentine and scrub in the basic composition, working with black and yellow.

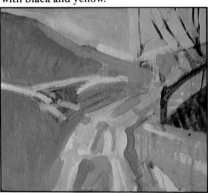

3. Thicken the paint and lighten the tone of the colors, adding cobalt blue and violet to the palette. Work quickly over the painting with broad brushstrokes.

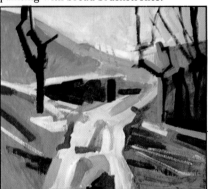

4. Develop the tonal contrast by drawing into the image with black and increasing the range of warm, light colors and mid-toned greens.

Highlighting · blocking in shapes

With a large bristle brush, the artist blocks in rough shapes of pale blue in the stream with thickish paint.

After drawing in the tree outlines in green, the artist is here working into the white areas between with a pale pink.

5. Work into the shapes of the trees with red and black and block in thick slabs of green, building up the texture by varying the quality of the brushmarks.

6. Use the point of a fine, round bristle brush to develop the linear structure of the composition and to color details. Paint in dark tones with ultramarine.

7. Elaborate the texture in the foreground with finely crosshatched brushstrokes of red, green and yellow woven across the previous work.

8. Give form and density to the foreground area with streaks and dabs of color. Add depth in the shadows with dark red and blue contrasted with white patterning.

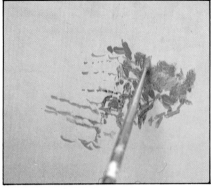

ONE HUNDRED YEARS ago, few artists would consider doing a landscape painting from anything other than the actual subject, *plein air* painting being synonymous with the great artists of the day. Today however, painting out of doors has become something of an anomaly and the artist is often looked upon as an object of curiosity. Most landscape painters learn through experience what is required to adapt themselves and their work to working out of doors. Choose your materials and equipment carefully and plan to be working under poor rather than perfect weather conditions. Do not bring a lot of materials with you; the fewer the better.

In this painting, the artist has purposely chosen a view with an interesting combination of colors and textures. The neutral, earth tones of the buildings work well with the leafy green forms of the trees, the touches of red and yellow are just strong enough to enliven general color areas.

A good point to keep in mind is that when working closely from the subject, it is not necessary to paint or draw exactly what you see before you. In this case the artist has chosen certain objects, shapes, and colors and used them to the advantage of the painting, sometimes exaggerating and sometimes underplaying colors and shapes to make the picture work as a harmonious unit.

1. Working from the center outward, draw in general subject outlines in pale blue with a No 3 bristle brush and begin to apply a thin raw umber tone.

2. Carry this same color outward from the center. Keep the paint consistency thin and work loosely.

Materials

Surface
Card sized with rabbit skin glue

Size
11.5in × 9in (29cm × 22.5cm)

Tools
No 3 bristle brush
Palette

Colors

Aureolin	Chrome green,
Black	Cobalt blue
Cadmium red light	Raw umber
Cadmium red medium	White
Cadmium yellow medium	Yellow ochre

Medium
Linseed oil
Turpentine

Touches of color · scratching back

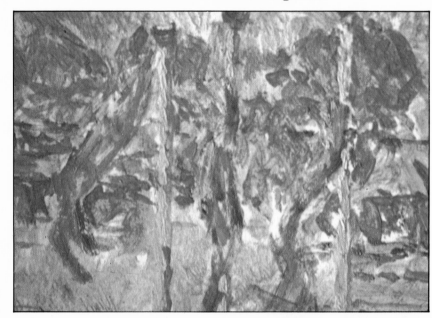

<u>Above</u>: Bright touches of color will often enliven an otherwise monochromatic painting. In this painting, the small red flag shapes add a valuable touch of interest to the finished picture.
<u>Right</u>: By scratching back through the wet paint with the end of a brush, an interesting texture can be obtained.

3. Put in basic horizontals and verticals in the blue used for the initial sketch. Carry green and brown tones over the painting. With cadmium red put in the flag shapes.

4. Mix chrome green, cadmium yellow and white. Thin with turpentine and loosely work in the foreground trees.

5. Continue over the painting developing lights and darks. Work back into previously painted areas and develop details.

WHETHER PAINTING OR drawing, few artists will work on a picture as a group of individual and independent parts. An artist will rarely begin in one corner and progress across the page, or complete a section without regard for the rest of the picture. There is sound reasoning behind this. While the artist may have a good idea of what the finished picture is to look like, it is impossible to predict exactly the result of each brushstroke and how it will affect the picture as a whole. There is a natural rhythm to painting which involves a constant checking and re-checking of the work – not only in a particular area, but in all areas simultaneously. As small and insignificant as one brushstroke may seem, it is impossible to put down a touch of color without it affecting every other color.

In studying the progression of the work shown here, the rhythm of work becomes clear. The artist mixes a color, applies a few touches, and with that same color moves to another part of the painting. The sky color is used not only in the sky, but in the trees and water as well. The purplish tone used as an underpainting is repeated throughout the painting in various shades and tones.

This is an efficient way of painting as it saves the artist from having to mix and match colors each time they are needed. More importantly, this method gives the picture unity which is not overt or obvious to the viewer. It is also the wisdom behind using a few colors and from those mixing other colors and tones. By limiting the palette to three or four colors, the artist is automatically ensuring that the painting will have harmony.

Materials

Surface
Prepared canvas board

Size
18in × 24in (45cm × 60cm)

Tools
Willow charcoal
Nos 2, 4 flat bristle brushes
Palette knives
Palette

Colors
Alizarin crimson	Cerulean blue
Cadmium red medium	Viridian
Cadmium yellow medium	White

Medium
Turpentine

1. Very lightly rough in the subject with willow charcoal. Block in the general color areas with a No 4 brush using tones of chrome green and violet.

2. With pure cerulean blue and a lighter shade of this (add white), put in water and tree highlights. Use cadmium yellow medium to describe the lighter tones.

3. With a No 2 brush, mix viridian green and white and develop the tree on the right using short, directional strokes.

4. Mix alizarin crimson and cadmium red medium and put touches in the green of the trees. Add white to this mixture and put in water highlights.

5. Lighten the blue-green shade used in the tree by adding white and carry this over into the water area. Lighten this mixture and block in the cloud shapes.

6. With a No 2 brush, mix cadmium yellow light and white and put in the sky tone. Carry this into the water, defining tree and sky reflections.

Overpainting · strengthening shapes

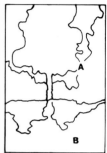

A. To strengthen the contrast between the tree outlines and the sky, the artist is here working with cadmium yellow and a small brush, working around tree shapes.

B. Overlaying the thin underpainting of the shadow areas in the water, the artist lays in short strokes of thick, undiluted paint.

Acrylic

PAINTING OR drawing cityscapes requires a different approach from the more traditional rural landscape picture. The artist may feel overwhelmed by the sheer scope of the subject and, from this incredible amount of information, what should be included in the picture. This is best determined by the goals of the artist and the techniques to be used. Very detailed and meticulous cityscapes, as seen for example in some primitive paintings, are as successful and interesting as more generalized, abstract scenes which include only basic shapes and little detail. One way to tackle the problem is to focus on a small area and include only broad, general areas to give an overall impression.

In the painting shown here, an image has been 'cut out' from a wider perspective. There is no horizontal plane in the immediate foreground and no view of the sky.

Start with a simple impression of geometric planes first outlined with a brush and then blocked in with a thin layer of color. You can then define the complexity of the structure gradually and work with thicker paint in small areas, describing local shapes and colors.

Materials

Surface
Stretched, primed canvas

Size
18in × 22in (45cm × 55cm)

Tools
No 3 and 5 flat bristle brush
Plate or palette

Colors
Black
Burnt sienna
Burnt umber
Cadmium red medium
Cadmium yellow medium

Cobalt blue
Hooker's green
Yellow ochre
White

Medium
Water

Blocking in shapes · using masking tape

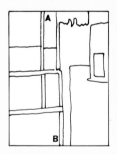

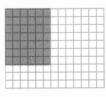

A. Working over the very thin underpainting, the artist begins to block in solid shapes of color with thick paint and small brush.

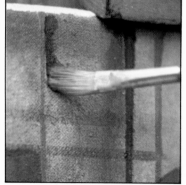

B. Masking tape may be used to create a clean, sharp edge. Make sure the surface is dry before putting down the tape and then work carefully into and over the tape with thickish paint. Peel off slowly and carefully to avoid smudging.

1. Draw up the general layout of the image in cobalt blue using a No 3 bristle brush. Lay in thin washes of color with a No 5 bristle brush.

2. Work over the whole canvas with a No 8 brush blocking in layers of thin color to show the basic shapes of trees and buildings. Reinforce with the No 3 brush.

3. Develop the structure of the drawing in cadmium red. Apply light washes of burnt umber and black to indicate shadows and depth.

4. Gradually build up the impression of form with small blocks of color, burnt umber, grey and yellow. Work into the trees with brown and green.

5. Continue to develop the form and color, drawing into the image in more detail with a No 3 brush. Thicken the paint and vary the direction of the strokes.

6. Lay in small shapes of color, adjusting the tonal balance to strengthen the qualities of light and shadow over the buildings.

7. Add to the details of the structure in the foreground, drawing the framework of steps and scaffolding in grey and black. Paint with the tip of the No 3 brush.

8. Increase the tonal depth of the colors by painting in shadow areas in burnt sienna and black. Work over the whole image revising shapes and tones.

9. Develop the linear forms in more detail with fine black lines. Strengthen the colors to build up the pattern of light and shade.

ALTHOUGH ACRYLICS ARE a relatively new phenomena in the painting world, their use has spread quickly, since they are flexible enough for use in most traditional types of painting. Their fast drying time and ability to be thinned to a watercolor-like consistency makes them ideal for the classical technique of overlaying thin areas of color one upon the other.

In the time of the Old Masters, almost all painting was done in this way. It is interesting to note that many of the Masters spent a great deal of their painting time developing the underpainting, and then working quickly through the final stages. Thus what is seen by the viewer in a Velazquez or Rubens are simply the last steps the artist took to complete the picture – with an elaborate underpainting lying just beneath the surface.

In this painting, the artist decided upon the mood of the picture before laying in the underpainting. As he wanted the painting to have a peaceful mood of a seascape at dusk, he chose a reddish underpainting, which would work well with the other colors used and give the entire picture a warmish tone. He has also used the traditional method of working from dark to light – slowly building up highlights from a dark base – and from the general to the specific.

Materials

Surface
Prepared canvas board

Size
26in × 24in (65cm × 60cm)

Tools
2B pencil
No 3 synthetic acrylic brush
Nos 2, 3, and 4 bristle brights
Nos 4 and 5 sable rounds
Mixing plates or palette
Jars for medium
Rags or tissues

Colors
Alizarin crimson   Cadmium yellow
Burnt sienna   Cobalt blue
Burnt umber   Pthalo blue
Cadmium green   Ultramarine blue
Cadmium red light   White

Medium
Water

1. Mix a fair amount of burnt sienna and water and apply quickly and loosely with a broad brush. In the foreground, use a drier mixture applied with short strokes.

3. Draw in verticals and horizontals of lighthouse and horizon with pencil. Mix chrome green and cadmium yellow medium and lay in small patches of grass.

5. Apply a darker wash of blue over the sky. Mix a light tone of white and ochre and put in the sea. Put in strong darks in burnt umber and details in foreground.

7. Mix alizarin crimson and burnt sienna and carefully put in the lighthouse stripes with a small brush.

2. Put in the lighthouse in a thin wash of the same burnt sienna. Cover the ground with a more opaque, darker tone. Mix alizarin crimson and brush in sky tone.

4. Mix thin wash of ultramarine and lay in the sky color. Letting previous layer dry, build up light foreground area with yellow ochre and white in a vertical direction.

6. Apply a very thin wash of pthalo blue for the sea. Overpaint burnt umber areas in chrome green and redefine highlights with yellow ochre and white.

8. Put in white highlights in the sea with a small sable brush and pure, undiluted white.

Dry-brush · lighthouse · sanding

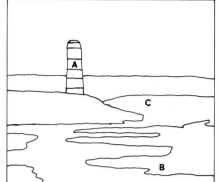

A. Using a broad bristle brush and cadmium red, the stripes in the lighthouse are defined, again allowing the underpainting to come through.

B. With a dry mixture of white and yellow ochre, the artist lets the brush drag across the dry paint surface to create texture.

C. With a piece of fine sandpaper, the artist smooths down the painting surface. This allows for fine, clear details to be put in without the interference of the textured surface.

1. Load a No 8 bristle brush with a mixture of gold ochre and raw umber. Work over the whole canvas indicating the basic forms of the landscape.

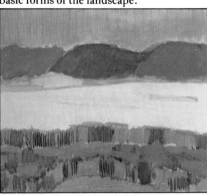

5. With a No 3 brush, work in more detail over the bright foreground colors with fine vertical and horizontal strokes of light and middle-toned greens.

A common practice with landscape artists is to make rough sketches. These include not only the subject but also notes concerning colors and lighting. The painting shown here is based upon the sketch made above. Note how the artist has included information on colors to be used.

MANY LANDSCAPE ARTISTS work out of doors on small pencil or watercolor sketches of the subject and return to the studio, using the drawings as reference material for larger paintings. This is far more convenient than attempting to carry cumbersome equipment from place to place; it also allows the artist to observe the subject closely and gather a great deal of information on form, color, changing light, and so on.

Acrylics were chosen as the medium for this painting in preference to oils because of their efficient covering power and drying speed which enable the painter to build up the composition rapidly with layers of color. There is more freedom than with other media because the opacity of the paint means that highlights and light colors can be applied at any stage over previous layers and a constant revision of tones and colors can be made.

The painting is enlivened by contrasts between detailed, active patches of pattern and strong color in the foreground; large flat areas of reflected light; and the horizontal bands of changing color.

Materials

Surface
Prepared canvas board

Size
24in × 20in (60cm × 50cm)

Tools
Nos 3, 6, 8 flat bristle brushes
No 4 sable brush
Plate or palette
Rags or tissues

Colors

Black	Olive green
Burnt umber	Raw umber
Cadmium yellow	Ultramarine blue
Chrome green	Vermilion
Cobalt blue	Viridian green
Gold ochre	White
Lemon yellow	

Medium
Water

Overlaying · broad areas

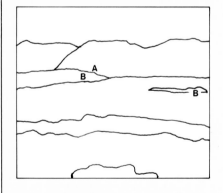

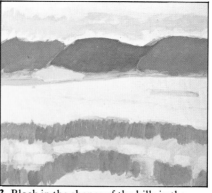

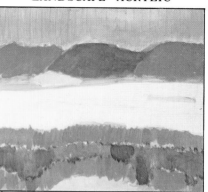

2. When dry, use a No 6 brush to lay in a warm, dark orange in the foreground and olive green above. Apply a thick layer of lemon yellow across the center.

3. Block in the shapes of the hills in the background in a green. Work into the foreground color with bright orange mixed from vermilion and yellow.

4. Using broad brush strokes, apply a light cobalt blue to form the basic tone of the sky, spreading the color with a rag. Work into the orange shapes with vivid green.

6. Build up the details with a variety of greens and greys, working with thin glazes of color and thick dabs of opaque paint.

7. Lift the tones in the foreground by adding small patches of light green and white applied with a sable brush, but do not cover the other colors completely.

8. Draw up detailed shapes in the background with the No 3 bristle brush using several shades of olive green.

(continued overleaf)

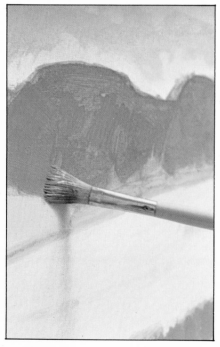

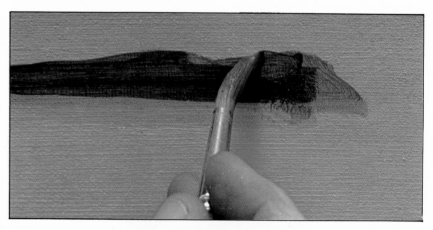

A. After the initial underpainting has been allowed to dry, the artist begins to block in broad areas of green in a thick, opaque paint.

B. Acrylics can be used in the traditional watercolor technique of layering thin washes of color. Here the artist is building up a dark area of chrome green and black by working over a darkish underpainting.

Sky tones · highlights

Showing the effective use of an underpainting to warm subsequent layers of color, the artist blocks in sky tones in light grey allowing the warm yellow underpainting to break through.

Using a vertical scrubbing motion, the artist is here putting in lighter shades of green in the foreground area.

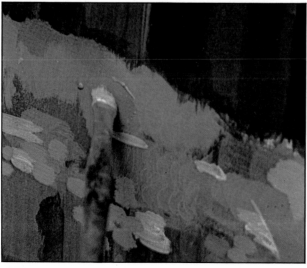

9. Lighten the tone of the sky and link the blue with a pale blue-green in the foreground. Add to the details with light orange, mixing in white to give opacity.

10. With a No 6 brush, scumble a layer of pale yellow across the sky area and work over it with light blue, grey and white, brushing the colors together vigorously.

11. Brighten the tone of the central field, laying a thick creamy yellow mixed from ochre, white and a touch of green.

12. Work into the foreground creating an area of small dabs of light green and white paint with the No 4 brush. Apply fine vertical strokes of dark green for contrast.

ACRYLIC IS ONE of the most flexible painting mediums in existence today. To make the most of it, the artist should become familiar with all of its many uses. A good way to familiarize yourself with the medium is to create a series of paintings, making a conscious effort to duplicate other media techniques. In this way you will learn what acrylics are capable of and how these techniques and painting methods can be effectively and harmoniously combined in one picture.

In this painting the artist has combined a number of different painting techniques to successfully capture and render the subject. The painting was begun using the traditional oil technique of underpainting. The artist continued to develop the picture using an assortment of brushes and techniques borrowed from other media. The wash, a traditional watercolor technique, was used to exploit the underpainting and create a subtlety of color tone; the paint was often used to 'draw' the subject and define specific areas of interest; in other areas a dryish paint mixture has been dragged across the surface in a texture similar to oil paint. This emphasizes that there are few rules in painting – especially when using acrylics – and that any techniques which serve to express the subject best can be used.

Materials

Surface
Stretched heavy white drawing paper

Size
23.5in × 20.5in (59cm × 51cm)

Tools
2B drawing pencil
No 4 synthetic acrylic brush
No 6 sable watercolour brush
Palette

Colors
Alizarin crimson   Cerulean blue
Black   Chrome green
Burnt sienna   White
Cadmium red medium   Yellow ochre

Medium
Water

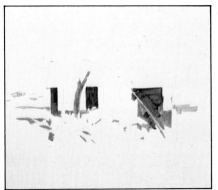

1. Having dampened and stretched a piece of paper, lightly sketch in the subject with pencil. Using a No 6 sable brush, lay in a wash of alizarin crimson and burnt sienna.

2. With the same brush, continue to block in the general subject shapes in burnt sienna, using the brush to 'draw' in the shapes. Keep the paint very wet.

3. Add a small amount of cadmium red to the burnt sienna and lay in the roof color. Put in the foreground with chrome green and yellow ochre.

4. Using a No 4 brush and pure chrome green, lay in the darker grass and shrub colors. Put in small touches of color in the tree with a short flicking motion.

5. Add a small amount of black to the chrome green and once dry, lay this over the previous grass and shrub areas. With alizarin crimson block in cloud shapes.

6. Mix white and cerulean blue and describe window shape. Carry the dark green tone into the tree. Mix chrome green and white and dab in grass.

7. Use this same light green to extend lighter grass areas and put in tree highlights. Put wash of burnt sienna in the foreground.

8. Cover foreground with light green tone of dryish consistency, allowing the brown underpainting to show through.

Underpainting

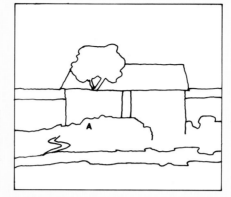

A. With a No 4 synthetic brush, the artist works over the painting laying in general dark areas. The white of the canvas is left bare for highlight areas.

Watercolor

WATERCOLOR IS ONE of the most versatile of drawing media. It can be handled with precision for fine detail work but is also naturally suited to a fluid and spontaneous style. You can exploit random effects in the flow and fall of the paint by spattering color from the end of the brush or blowing the thin, wet washes into irregular rivulets across the paper. Integrate these marks with carefully controlled brushwork to vary the textures in the painting.

The full effect of watercolor depends upon luminous, transparent washes of color built up layer upon layer. As white paint deadens the freshness of color, small areas of highlight are achieved by leaving the white paper bare while light tones are produced by using thin washes of color. Dark tones are slowly brought to a suitable intensity by the use of several successive applications of thin layers of the same color.

The urn shape was initially protected with a layer of masking fluid, painted carefully into the outline. This seals off the paper while the rest of the surface is freely painted over with large brushes and watery paint. When the work is complete and dry you can then rub off the mask and work on shadows and highlights of the shape with a small brush.

Materials

Surface
Heavy stretched paper

Size
23in × 20in (40cm × 50cm)

Tools
2B pencil
No 6 sable round brush
No 10 ox-eye round brush
1in (2.5cm) decorators' brush
Masking fluid

Colors
Burnt umber	Hooker's green
Cadmium red medium	Ivory black
Chrome green	Payne's grey
Cobalt blue	Yellow ochre

1. Sketch in the basic lines of the drawing with a pencil, carefully outlining the shape of the urn. Paint in this shape with masking fluid and let it dry completely.

2. Use a No 10 ox-eye brush to lay a broad light wash of cobalt blue across the top half of the painting and chrome green and Payne's grey across the foreground.

3. Mix a dark, neutral grey and paint wet streaks of color to form the trunks of the trees. Blow the wet paint in strands across the paper making a network of branches.

4. As the paint dries, work over the structure with green, grey and umber rolling the brush into the pools of paint and letting the color spread.

5. Load a decorators' brush with paint and flick tiny spots of colour into the washes. Block in the shape of the wall with a thin layer of red and brown using a No 6 brush.

6. Work over the foreground with the decorators' brush loaded with Hooker's green, using a rough, scrubbing motion. Draw in details on the wall.

7. Let the painting dry completely. Gently rub away the masking fluid with your finger – make sure all the fluid is off and try not to damage the paper.

8. Paint in the shadows on the urn in brown and grey, adding a little yellow ochre and light red to warm the tones. Paint the form and stonework.

Masking fluid · spattering · blotting · stippling

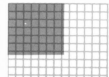

To create a spattered effect, load a large bristle brush with paint and quickly run your finger or a small knife through the hairs.

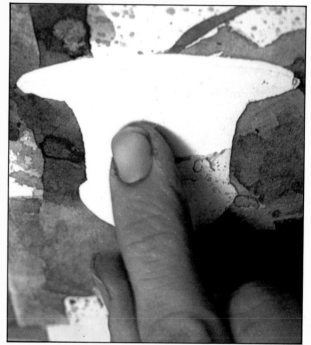

An alternative to spattering paint is to stipple with the end of a broad bristle brush. Here the artist is using a decorators' brush to lay in small dots of color.

A dense, leafy texture can be achieved by blotting a wet area with a piece of tissue. Do not rub but simply put the tissue down, press, and pick it up to leave small gaps and crevices in the paint surface.

Masking fluid may be used to protect the white paper from the paint. When the painting is completed, rub off the fluid with your finger. If the fluid is put on with a brush, make sure to rinse the brush immediately after use.

THE TECHNIQUES REQUIRED for this type of painting are quite lengthy and it is advisable to practise on scraps of a similar paper before beginning the actual painting.

A large, wet pool of color will dry with a gradated tone and strong, irregular outline. Overlaying a succession of washes produces vivid colors, a patterned network of light and dark tones, and linear detail suggesting the texture of foliage and flowers. You can speed up the drying process with a hairdryer or fan but, since this tends to deaden the color, it is best to let the painting dry naturally.

The image is built up in the traditional watercolor technique of working from light to dark. Start by laying in pale tones in thin, broad washes leaving patches of white paper to form highlight areas. Because the paint is so fluid, only one good-quality, medium-sized sable brush is needed. Make broad sweeps of watery color with the bristles loose or spread, and bring the tip to a point for finer details. Study each shape carefully and draw directly with the brush. Color can be lifted from the surface with a clean, damp Q-tip to lighten the tones. Detailed corrections are difficult with this type of painting, but it is possible to make small corrections by rubbing the surface when completely dried with a fine-grained sandpaper.

Materials

Surface
Stretched white cartridge paper

Size
13in × 8in (32cm × 20cm)

Tools
HB pencil
No 6 round sable brush
Plate or palette
Q-tips

Colors
Alizarin crimson	Emerald green
Black	Prussian blue
Burnt sienna	Scarlet lake
Cadmium yellow	Viridian
Cobalt blue	Yellow ochre

Medium
Water

1. Sketch out the composition very lightly with an HB pencil. Lay washes of thin wet paint to establish basic forms and local colors.

2. Work over the painting again with light washes blocking in more shapes. Let the colors run together in patches to create a soft, fuzzy texture.

Cleaning with knife · sanding · blotting

Where paint has inadvertently splashed on the white surface, the artist can very carefully scratch it off with a knife.

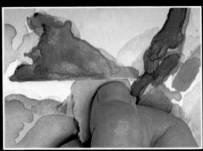

After scraping off spots or splashes, the artist is here very lightly sanding the surface with a fine grade sandpaper. Use a very light touch.

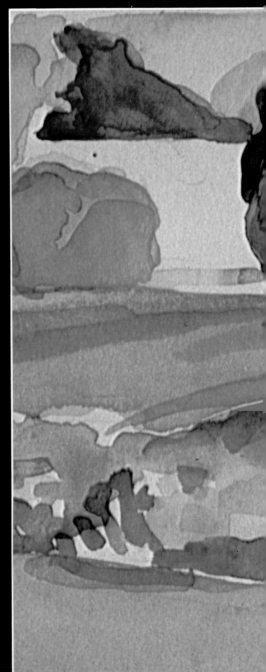

3. Let the painting dry and then apply layers of denser color, gradually building up the forms with thin overlays.

4. Paint in the shadow shapes over the grass with broad streaks of blue and green. Work into the trees with overlapping areas of colour to show the form.

5. Strengthen dark tones in the background with Prussian blue and black. Lay a broad wash of yellow over the grass to lift the tone.

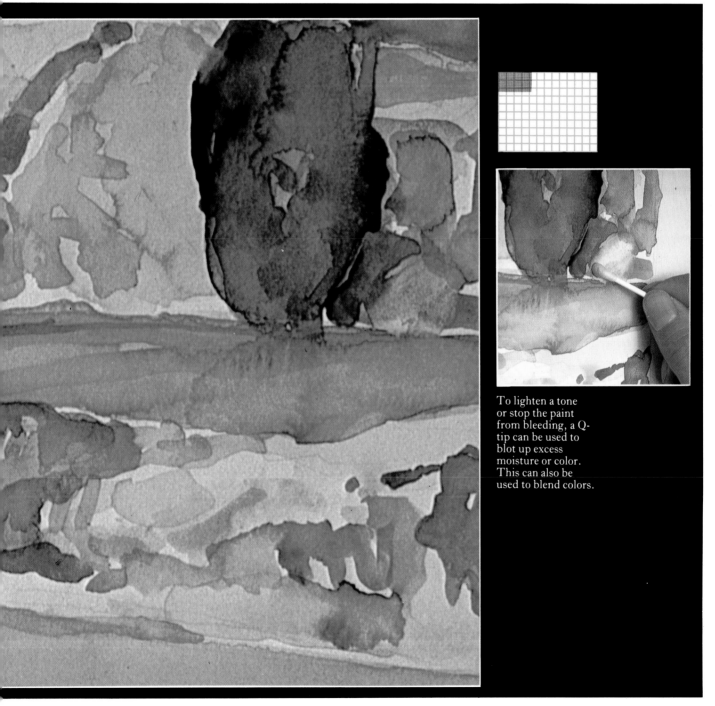

To lighten a tone or stop the paint from bleeding, a Q-tip can be used to blot up excess moisture or color. This can also be used to blend colors.

THE PAINTING SHOWN here captures a sense of distance by showing how the land recedes gradually from the foreground towards the horizon and using the two trees as a central focus. This is achieved by carefully varying color tones – placing strong, warm hues in the foreground and colors which are cooler and less intense in the distance. The impression of receding space is enhanced by the sky gradually lightening and finally rising into a thin strip of white where the paper is left bare.

To keep an overall coherence to the picture, the colors in each area are subtly linked together. For example, the same blue has been used for the linear details in the middle distance as in the shadow areas of the trees. A harmonious balance of warm and cool tones has been applied as seen in the contrast between the warm brown of the foreground, the colder yellow across the center of the painting, and the reddish-brown and blue tones in the trees which deepen the intensity of the green washes.

Materials

Surface
Heavy, stretched paper

Size
16in × 11in (40cm × 27cm)

Tools
Nos 6, 8 sable round brushes
Large sable blending brush

Colors
Burnt umber	Scarlet lake
Emerald green	Ultramarine blue
Gamboge yellow	Viridian
Payne's grey	Yellow ochre
Prussian blue	

Medium
Water

1. First wet the paper using a large No 8 brush dipped in water. Lay in a thin wash of Prussian blue with a No 8 sable brush, working down from the top of the paper.

2. Brush in a yellow ochre wash across the centre of the paper, leaving white space along the horizon line and in areas where the main forms will be placed.

3. Use viridian, emerald green and burnt umber to apply the basic forms of the trees, indicating areas of light and shade.

4. Draw into the shapes of the trees in more detail with the point of a No 6 brush. Darken the burnt umber with a little blue and mix yellow into the greens.

5. Continue to extend the forms and intensify the colors. Fan out the bristles of a No 8 brush between thumb and forefinger to draw feathery texture.

6. Dampen the yellow ochre wash with clean water and draw into it with a mixture of Payne's grey and blue.

7. Add detail into the grey area with ultramarine, keeping the paint thin and wet. Use the same blue in foliage shadows and contrast with a warm reddish brown.

8. Mix up Payne's grey with burnt umber and lay a broad streak of color across the foreground with a No 8 sable brush, working directly onto the dry paper.

Dry-brush · the wash

A consistent, even wash can be achieved by mixing a large amount of paint and water in a small dish; dip a large sable brush into this and move across the surface with an even pressure.

To effectively use the dry-brush technique, load a brush with paint, blot on a rag and grasping the brush hairs between the thumb and fingers, flick the brush on the surface to create a feathery texture.

Gouache

THIS PAINTING demonstrates an innovative and imaginative method of combining gouache with another water-based medium – ink – to create an individual and expressive seascape. There is nothing innovative in the use of an underpainting in itself, but it is not generally used with water-based media such as watercolor or gouache due to the inherent transparency of these media. In this instance, the artist has first executed an underpainting in bold, primary colors, which serves to unify the painting and help eliminate the inevitable chalkiness of gouache.

Since the more traditional method of underpainting requires time-consuming layering of color upon color, the use of these bold colors for the underpainting expedites the painting process. In this method, the artist can jump directly from the underpainting to developing the basic structure of the painting without having to wait for previous coats to dry.

While opaque and flat, gouache retains many of the qualities of all water-based paints and can be worked wet-into-wet, spattered, or dry-brushed. The artist has here used a combination of all of these techniques which, when combined with a subtle mixture of color and tone – all of which are enhanced by the initial underpainting – results in an evocative and atmospheric painting.

Materials

Surface
Stretched watercolor paper

Size
19in × 17in (47cm × 42.5cm)

Tools
Nos 4, 6, 10 sable brushes
Palette or mixing plate
Tissues or rags

Colors

Gouache:	Colored inks:
Black	Black
Burnt umber	Blue
Olive green	Green
Payne's grey	Orange
Prussian blue	Red
White	

Medium
Water

Underpainting with ink · details

The very bold colors of an underpainting done in colored inks will later be modified by opaque gouache. Here, in the first step, (below) the inks are bleeding into one another.

In the final steps,
the artist puts in
small details of pure
black gouache with a
small sable brush.

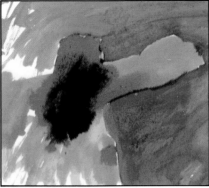

1. With a No 10 brush, lay down broad areas of red, orange, blue and green ink corresponding to the shapes and color tones of the subject.

2. While still wet, mix a variety of grey tones from white, olive green, and Payne's grey gouache. Very loosely rough in the pier allowing the ink and gouache to bleed.

3. With a No 4 brush, begin to dot in lighter tones of grey and white, once again allowing the colors to bleed together.

4. Cover the orangish underpainting in the foreground with a thin wash of burnt umber.

5. Add a touch of olive green to the white, Payne's grey, and green mixture and with the No 10 brush cover the sky and sea area with broad, loose strokes.

6. Cover the remaining sky area in this same color and let dry. Using pure white gouache, block in white shape to left and small touches of white in the foreground.

7. Add more olive green to the mixture and loosely put in strokes in sea and foreground rocks. Put pure white on a No 4 brush and spatter.

8. With a No 4 brush and black gouache, put in the fine details of the picture.

NO ONE MEDIA can completely capture the diverse and subtle range of colors to be found in nature; the total effect is created by the relationships of all the colors together and the influence of light. Even if a landscape is predominantly green, there are a multitude of tones and hues within the one color to be identified and translated onto the painting surface. A low-key green, for example, may be caused by a subtle cast of blue or red and the painting will be livelier if these contrasts are exploited or exaggerated.

As a general rule, remember that colors in the foreground are the most intense and fade towards the horizon. Within this range there are shifts between warm and cool tones; these help to establish form and position in the overall scheme of the painting.

Only one brush and a limited color range have been used for this painting; the variety of hues and tones is due to careful, observant color mixing. As gouache is thick and opaque, be careful not to overmix the colors. The paint can be laid in thin washes of color or thickly daubed depending on how much water is added.

Materials

Surface
Stretched heavy cartridge paper

Size
14.5in × 18in (36cm × 45cm)

Tools
No 6 round sable brush

Colors
Brilliant green	Cobalt blue
Black	Scarlet
Cadmium yellow	White

Medium
Water

1. Paint in soft shapes to show trees, sky and water using thin washes of blue and green adding white to vary the tone.

2. Work into these colors with darker tones to establish the basic forms and give the impression of distance.

3. With undiluted paint, overpaint the forms in detail, varying the green hues by adding touches of yellow or red. Intensify the colors in the reflections on the water.

4. Mix brown from scarlet and black and draw up the trunk and branches of the tree. Extend the shape of the tree working with small dabs of red, green and orange.

5. Increase the contrast in the light and dark colors over the whole image. Work into the foreground with horizontal and vertical stripes of blended color.

6. Heighten the tones with small patches of thin paint over the sky and trees, mixing white into the colors.

Highlighting

Working over a
partially dry
underpainting, the
artist puts in a
highlight tone.

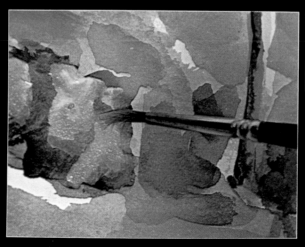

Pastel

WHILE PASTELS are generally considered a drawing medium, working with them involves both painting and drawing skills. The same principles apply to pastels as to many painting media as seen in the overlaying of colors to create new colors and transparency.

The main difference between using pastel and the usual painting media is that the former cannot be easily erased or corrected. The artist's only recourse to correcting a pastel drawing is to overlay more color. For this reason the picture should be developed through careful and well thought-out layering of tone and color rather than through heavy and dense application of the pastels.

In this picture the artist has used some elements of the pointillist technique without the use of 'points'. Rather, thin strokes of pure color have been laid down beside and on top of one another to give the impression of mixing colors and tones. The picture is based primarily on the use of warm and cool colors – red and blue – and their interraction with one another. By careful use of complementary colors, such as a touch of a reddish tone in a predominantly blue area, a dull and predictable picture is avoided. Close examination of the finished picture reveals that where there is a large area of one color – blue for example – its complement, red, has been added to give the picture unity. The complementary color also 'bounces off' the other warm color areas, unifying the picture as a whole.

Materials

Surface
Heavy weight pastel paper

Size
18.5in × 26in (46cm × 65cm)

Tools
Willow charcoal
Rags or tissues
Fixative

Colors
Blue-green	Light red
Cobalt blue	Light yellow
Crimson	Orange
Dark blue	Pale blue
Dark green	Yellow

1. With broad strokes, lay in the basic warm and cool colors as an underpainting.

2. With heavier, linear strokes, begin to develop darker tones of these general color areas moving over the paper with one color at a time.

3. Begin to lay in lighter, warmer tones of orange, yellow, and red building up the color contrasts of the warm-cool, blue-red motif. Keep the strokes light.

4. Return to the dark colors previously used, heightening shadow areas with a heavier stroke.

5. With cobalt blue, lighten any areas which appear too heavy or dark. Put in the sky with pale blue.

6. Return to the dark blue, red, and green colors to put in the final touches of emphasis and contrast using stroke to give direction and shape.

Overlaying pure color

With pastel, the artist produces colors which mix optically on the surface by applying thin lines of pure color one over the other. Here, pale blue strokes are laid over crimson in the wall to create an impression of purple.

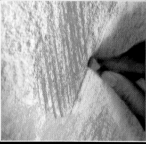 

WORKING WITH OIL pastels requires a slightly different approach and attitude than using the traditional chalk type of pastel. Unlike chalk pastels, oil pastels can be used as a painting medium. They can be softened and mixed on a palette and then directly applied to the surface with a palette knife; or thinned with turpentine and then wiped onto the surface with a rag. Pastels of any type are difficult to correct, and oil pastels more difficult than most. Without the aid of turpentine, a rag, and some heavy rubbing, the strokes you put down are permanent. For this reason, use a fairly light touch in the preliminary stages of the drawing.

In this painting, the artist has used a variety of techniques to exploit the medium's potential to its fullest and has literally painted with the pastels using all the techniques normally ascribed to traditional oil painting.

Due to their rich and thick texture, another effective technique is to scratch back through the pastel to reveal the original surface color. This can be achieved with any sharp tool to create a variety of lines and tones from a dense crosshatching to a light and flowing line.

Materials

__Surface__
Stretched, strong cartridge paper

__Size__
9in × 7in (22cm × 17.5cm)

__Tools__
2B pencil
Palette knife
Q-tips
Rags or tissues
Pen knife

__Oil pastel colors__

Black	Ultramarine blue
Cerulean blue	White
Payne's grey	

__Medium__
Turpentine

1. Make a preliminary sketch in pencil of the main features and compositional structure of the picture.

2. At this point, do not worry about the details of the picture, but loosely rough in the basic sea, sky, and land colors with loose, diagonal strokes.

3. Cover this layer with a thick, opaque white and shades of grey. Blend with a palette knife, pressing hard into the surface. Scratch back with edge of knife.

4. Over this, lay in the dark areas of the sky and horizon with ultramarine blue. Create foreground waves with white applied in short strokes.

Using the palette knife · blending

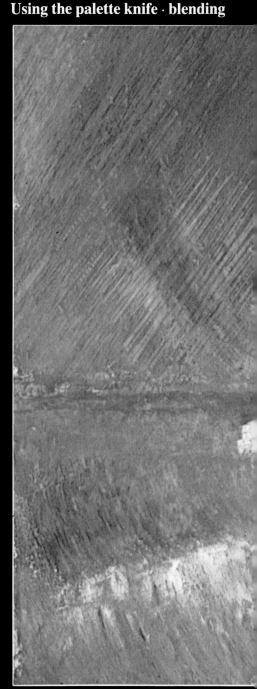

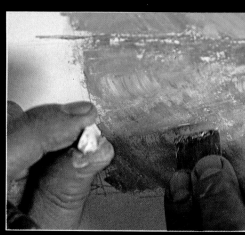

5. Dip a Q-tip in turpentine and blend the pastel over the entire picture surface to cover any remaining white areas.

6. Put a darker grey in the sky, using diagonal strokes. Lay in light areas of waves and land with white, or scratch back to white of surface with a knife.

7. Heighten the contrast in the foreground waves by adding more directional strokes of dark grey.

Here the artist is seen pressing small pieces of oil pastel onto the surface with a broad palette knife. The knife, like a brush, can be used to create directional strokes and textures.

With a Q-tip dipped in turpentine, the artist works over the oil pastel surface, blending colours and covering white gaps in the surface.

8. Add deeper blue touches around the white of the wave crests to heighten this contrast.

Pencil

COLORED PENCILS have a special relevance to landscape drawing, especially when the artist wishes to depict the effects of sun and shadow. The variety of lights and darks which can be achieved with colored pencils allows the artist to either work with a very pale and delicate range of colors and tone, or with a very intense and bold palette. When the two are combined – a pale, loose stroke and an intense and colorful area – the effect is balanced yet dynamic. In this case, the combination of architecture and nature is well suited to the medium, and vice versa.

Much like painting media, colored pencils allow the artist to build up layer upon layer of subtle color to create a transparent effect. For instance, crosshatching in different colors – overlaying one area of colored strokes over another color – can create an interesting tone and texture in the picture.

Drawing with colored pencil requires patience and thoroughness. The point of the pencil being relatively small, it is difficult to cover large areas with any evenness of tone and stroke. A smooth, hardish paper or board is normally used with pencil work, however, a roughly textured surface can create interesting white 'gaps' and grainy effects.

Materials

Surface
Stretched, rough drawing paper

Size
30in × 25in (75cm × 62.5cm)

Tools
Eraser
Pencil sharpener or small knife

Colors
Cerulean blue	Light yellow
Chrome green	Medium yellow
Dark brown	Ultramarine blue
Dark green	Yellow ochre

1. After sketching in general shapes with blue pencil, develop general shadow areas with blue and brown pencils.

3. Put in dark areas with black and dark brown pencils. Crosshatch using different colors and directional strokes to create color and tone.

5. Carry the light yellow and ochre tones into the foreground and palm tree.

7. Put in very loose strokes of brown in the middle distance. With a strong stroke, develop the green of the foreground palm. Highlight very bright areas with white.

2. With a pale yellow pencil, begin to put in the lighter areas of the wooden structure. This 'underpainting' will ensure a feeling of bright daylight.

4. Work from the centre outward to maintain the picture's focal point. Build up shapes using ultramarine blue for the darker areas.

6. Build up a strong, detailed drawing of the foreground palm with pale and dark green tones.

8. Carry loose, blue strokes over the foreground to indicate shadow.

Palm textures · overlaying dark colors · developing shadows

Working around the shape of the far dome, the artist overlays a dark green area with light green strokes.

In the initial steps, the artist begins to block in areas of dark color as in the windows of the house.

To create the texture of a palm tree, the artist overlays thin strokes of color.

BECAUSE PAINTING equipment is often difficult and cumbersome to manage out of doors, many landscape artists prefer to do rough sketches which are later used as reference for paintings. However, many landscape drawings are interesting as pictures in their own right.

The drawing shown has many qualities both in terms of pencil technique and subject which are worth noting. Notice that the artist has chosen a strong vertical space in which to draw. This is not typical of most landscape work which is generally done in the 'landscape', or horizontal position. The picture itself, however, is described using horizontal strokes which serves to create an interesting contrast between the shape of the overall image and the image itself.

A putty eraser is very effective in creating highlights. After the general tones have been laid down, the artist can work into the picture erasing out light or highlight areas. These can later be modified by working over again in pencil, or strengthened by further erasing.

Materials

Surface
Cartridge paper

Size
6in × 18in (15cm × 45cm)

Tools
2B, 4B pencils
Putty eraser
Fixative

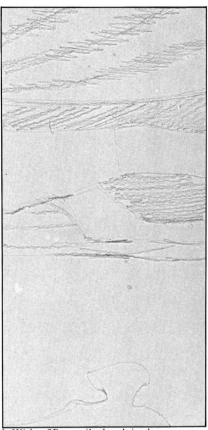

1. With a 2B pencil, sketch in the perimeter of the drawing and very lightly block in the sky and land shapes.

2. With a 4B pencil, block in the foreground tone and work into darker areas. Keep the strokes loose and light.

3. Work back into the clouds with the same pencil developing a stronger tone.

4. Using the tip of a putty eraser, work over cloud shapes using the same directional strokes as used with the pencil.

Erasing

After erasing out highlight areas, the artist returned to the drawing with the 4B pencil to work into dark areas and redefine outlines.

DRAWING IS IN many ways similar to sculpture. The sculptor, while carving out a shape, is always concerned with the space around the shape – the 'holes' which the observer will see through. This is known as negative space; a concept often difficult to grasp but essential to the success of a drawing or painting, especially when the artist wishes to exploit the use of 'white space' or the blank paper.

The drawing shown here is an excellent example of the use of negative and white space. While the artist used the pencils to create an image, he has also used the white of the paper to emphasize shapes and areas between and around the forms. An example is the thin line of red placed diagonally behind the plants. The observer reads this as a 'wall'; no more than this simple line is needed to create the impression of space and depth.

The picture also shows that the entire surface need not be covered to create an effective drawing. If you imagine the picture with all the white areas filled in, you would see that the drawing would lose much of its graphic impact. It takes practice to know when to stop a drawing. Very often the impact of a drawing can be lessened or lost if overworked or carried too far.

Materials

Surface
Smooth, heavy weight drawing paper

Size
23.5in × 17in (59cm × 42cm)

Tools
B, 2B, 4B drawing pencils
Eraser
Ruler

Colors

Black	Dark green
Blue-green	Light green
Dark grey	Red

1. Very lightly sketch in a small area of the subject with a 2B pencil and begin to define leaf shapes and background with dark green and black, pressing firmly.

2. Using a diagonal stroke, carry the dark green color on to the next area, lightly hatching in the area and then reworking. Put in red line with ruler.

3. Continue to work around this small area, defining the palm leaves in tones of grey and green, first working lightly and then building up heavier, detail areas.

4. Work back into previous areas with black and green pencils, strengthening the darks with a heavy, dense stroke.

5. With blue-green and dark green, begin to put in the cactus shape.

Finished picture · underdrawing

In order to successfully balance the composition of the drawing, in the last step the artist described the palm tree on the far right. Note that only pale colors and a light touch were used; the tree serves to balance the picture but does not overwhelm the left hand side.

With a light blue pencil, the artist is here putting in the first layer of color which will later be developed by overlaying different colors.

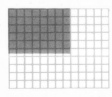

Pen and ink

PEN AND INK has a long tradition in both landscape and architectural drawing. It is especially well suited for the latter as a variety of lines and textures can be created without losing the linear qualities inherent in a cityscape. It is a good medium for working out of doors as well. With pen, pad, and bottle of ink, the artist can situate himself anywhere for either quick sketching or detailed drawing.

Ink is a very flexible medium and can be used in a variety of ways. The usual technique is to use only the pen, nib, and ink; this in itself will provide you with an unlimited choice in terms of line and tone. In this instance, the artist has chosen the traditional use of line for the initial sketch only and has proceeded to develop the picture through the use of innovative and unconventional tools. A thumb can be used to create unusual shadows and textures; the side of a box, when dipped in ink and pressed on to the surface gives an intriguing 'architectural' effect. Spattering the ink with a toothbrush will create a fine mist similar to an aquatint.

If working out of doors there may be many interesting objects around you which can be used in a similar fashion – drawing with a stick, 'printing' with a leaf, dipping some grass in ink and drawing it across the page.

Materials

Surface
Smooth, white cartridge paper

Size
16.5in × 12in (41cm × 30cm)

Tools
Pen holder	Toothbrush
Fine and medium nibs	Small knife
Masking tape	Small box

Colors
Black waterproof India ink

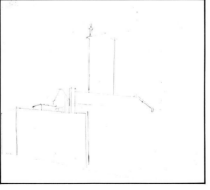

1. Begin by directly sketching in the main verticals and horizontals of the picture with a fine nib.

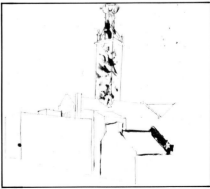

2. Use the back of the pen to create a thick, emphatic line. The thumb can be used to develop an interesting shadow texture as in the tower.

Finished picture · blotting with finger · spattering

In the last step, the artist put in very faint cloud shapes. This was accomplished by tearing pieces of paper and using their rough edges as a mask over which a fine mist of ink was spattered. Very light lines were then put in to define the shapes. Details were then re-emphasized.

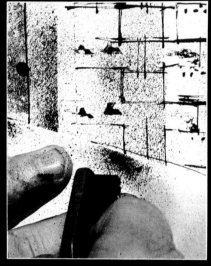

To create a spattered effect, dip a toothbrush in ink and, masking the area not to be spattered with a piece of paper, draw a finger quickly through the brush bristles.

Dipping a finger in ink and blotting it on to the surface creates an interesting texture. In this case, the sharp, crisp lines of the tower work well with the greyish smudges caused by the finger.

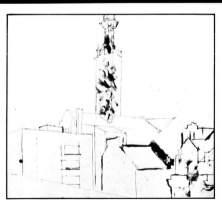

3. Use the back of the pen to develop the foreground objects. Dip the end of a small box in ink and press lightly to the surface for a brick-like effect.

4. Build up dark areas by defining geometric shapes and details with a medium nib.

5. Dip a toothbrush in ink and mask the area not to be covered with tape. Run a knife blade quickly over the brush to create spatters.

WHEN USING the traditional pen, nib, and ink it is important to note that it is basically a linear form of rendering. The marks are definite and not easily erased, and 'colors' must be created by hatched and scribbled strokes rather than blending. It is important to understand such characteristics and limitations which will enable you to focus your attention on aspects of the subject which lend themselves to the descriptive qualities of the medium.

When working in pen and ink, look for a subject with a strong, linear emphasis, well-defined motifs and dense pattern or texture. A good range of colored inks is available; there is no need to consider this a primarily monochrome medium. The colors form the intermediary tones between black and the clear white of the paper. Until you feel confident in handling color, however, it may be well to restrict yourself to a few basic tones.

Start by roughing out a simple linear framework for the drawing and then work into each area in detail, gradually building up the overall pattern. Develop a range of marks which correspond to the natural forms and textures without trying to reproduce every shape in detail. As the work progresses, adjust the density of the colors and patterns to achieve a satisfactory tonal balance.

Materials

Surface
White cartridge paper

Size
18.5in × 26in (46cm × 65cm)

Tools
Thick, square-nibbed pen
Fine mapping pen

Colors
April green	Deep green
Black	Sunshine yellow

1. Draw up the general outline of the image in black ink using a large, broad-nibbed pen. Indicate the main elements with fluid, linear strokes.

2. Work over the whole image again in black starting to define the shapes and forms in detail, using thick and thin nibs.

3. Build up a textured surface to suggest the grass with scratchy, criss-crossed marks, overlaying green and black.

4. Draw into the large tree in black, making heavy shadows with broad pen strokes. Work over the black with green and yellow.

5. Contrast the strong black textures with a thin layer of green crosshatching in the background. Draw with a fine pen using quick, light strokes.

6. Fill in the central area of grass and leaves with a woven pattern of green and black marks. Draw together the separate sections of the image.

Outlining

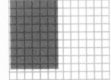

With a broad-nibbed pen, the artist is here putting in the general outlines of the picture. The width of the line is varied by turning the pen while drawing.

FINE, LINEAR DRAWING with pen and ink requires a careful, deliberate approach. Tonal shading must be developed gradually and crosshatching cannot be rapidly blocked in. The crisp, emphatic lines of a pen drawing have no equivalent and it is worthwhile to acquire the skill and patience to handle the pen to produce the dramatic, graphic effects of this medium.

This drawing gives a general impression of a landscape by starting with a loose sketch which outlines shapes and positions of trees and bushes. Each area of hatched lines and irregular, scribbled marks correspond to the basic tonal and textural structure. While the elements are treated separately, the whole image is constantly considered as a whole and brought together in the final stages.

Your technique should be controlled but not rigid – keep the pen well charged with ink and make decisive, fluid strokes. Even if the drawing is quite small, the marks should be as vigorous as possible, since it is texture, not color, which provides visual interest. Keep a lively balance in the tones by working some areas more densely than others and by varying the direction of the strokes and character of the marks.

Materials

Surface
Thick white cartridge paper

Size
12in × 8in (30cm × 20cm)

Tools
HB pencil
Dip pen
Medium nib

Colors
Black waterproof India ink

1. Make a light sketch of the layout with an HB pencil. Start to draw with the pen showing rough outlines and tones.

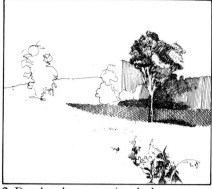

2. Develop the tones using the large tree as a focal point and working outwards. Build up the texture with fluid scribbled marks and crisp lines.

Crosshatching tones

3. Work across the paper sketching in shapes and elaborating forms.

4. Extend the hatched tones, establishing receding planes and overall shape of the image. Develop details in the foreground with small, irregular patterns.

5. Concentrate on details, particularly in the foreground, and work over the outlines of the shapes to soften the contours.

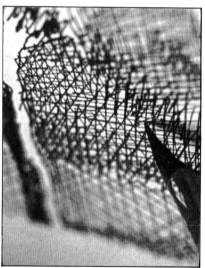

This detail of the shadow area behind the tree shows the artist using crosshatching to develop dense and varied tonal areas.